JOURNAL OF MY HEART

Journal of My Heart

LETTERS TO MY FAMILY PART I

Irene Cunningham

Superior Publishing LLC.

Contents

This book is dedicated to my family.
I love you all more than you know.

1

I Want My Family to Understand

My story of God's unconditional love and the the true unending, empathetic love of my husband, lover and friend.

I am sooo hopeful that my family can really realize how we were raised in true unconditional love. We were taught that family is everything and GRACE begins at home and spreads abroad!!

I feel blessed to have a voice and blessed with a man who does not stifle me, but I feel sometimes I speak out too much. Sometimes, I do feel I am too vocal or outspoken. But when God says to me, "Speak to that young girl or boy because she or he is brave to tell what she or he is really feeling or have going on." It could destroy our black families if we don't speak out on it in Jesus name. And also tell our children we are proud of them, and we love them in spite of good or bad.

I have not worked as an RN for 20+ years and GOD gave me a man of GOD who did not, has not and will not be moved. I am the product of a soldier DESSIE PAYNE AND A KING EUGENE PAYNE and even though he liked the women he always came back home to that strong woman!!! She said never leave your kids no matter who says so or who leaves!! She not only taught me that growing up but she showed me how to stay. And if she stayed with 9 children I knew God would see me through everything!

My mother taught me how to be a strong black woman, work hard, and you can have and accomplish whatever it is you want to in life.

2

December 24, 2008
JOURNAL
INTRODUCTION

8:40 P.M. This is the beginning of the book I had said I wanted to write about my life. As the wife of a strong, wonderful, God-fearing man, and the mother of three beautiful, black children, all of whom I love and adore and for whom I still live!!!!

I love y'all
Mom & Wife

When does your life begin?

Journal Title: When Does Your Life Begin?

WHEN?

WHY?

WHERE?

When does your life begin is a question I often ask myself?

When are you going to really do you?

Why do you still have empathy for others but they have none for you?

Where is the time to follow your dreams?

And how do you truly let your heart break and how to find yourself and do whatever you want to do, and have for your future?

Instead of being children, we had to stay with granny at night, when we were growing up, and be scared. We would be scared out of our eight and ten year old minds because granny was crazy and paranoid due to organic brain syndrome. Now it's known as, "Alzheimer's". We were lost in fear and anxiety because caring for our 80 year old grandmother should not have been our responsibility.

Can you even imagine the"bad nerves" as my mom would say? Grandma had bad nerves and she was meticulous about her house being clean, talk about O.C.D., P.T.S.D. etc. That was what we were raised under. Our history precedes us. Your childhood is who you are. We were children of, share cropper, on my father's side of the family, and the Underground Railroad mom's side. My mom's uncle, killed a white man and my granny side, their brother killed his son. Rules had to be followed, we were taught to respect our elders, honor thy mother and father and please do not abuse or fight your parents!!

My mom used to say, "The first time you hit your mother you're going to have to fight me every time I see you. I believed her too. She and dad were my heroes. They worked hard manual jobs and had businesses.

Written on an unknown date.

Mr. Joseph Cunningham

September 2019

    You know what? When everything is said and done and all the fake friends and family are not around to support me who is left? No one, but my God in heaven and my first and last love, who was and is my strength, my backbone, my man, my lover, my friend, and my husband, Mr. Joseph Cunningham. There is no one like him who loves me unconditionally with all of my weaknesses and my stuff. Baby I hope to be the woman that you deserve for the rest of my life as we grow old together in love. As I grow older, I am beginning to see that my life was spent working like a dog for twenty years, taking care of others in my extended family and helping my husband. The hope is that we have a good life and make sure our family is good and move on. But at the end of the day if these terms of endearment is not reciprocated to you, be able to take that feeling of being left to fight your battle alone while everyone else moves on with their lives. I do forever thank God for my boo, he is my better half because he makes me want to do better. So we can have an even better life, especially during our retirement years.

Thanks Bae this was recorded September 2019

3

Losing Sabrina

When my little girly died, I was so heartbroken and I just laid in bed and cried day in and day out. My mom would say, " you have to pray." And I was praying for God to relieve my pain and heal my baby. And after she died, I blamed myself for her being sick. At the age of 18, I did not know any better than to blame myself. I did not receive any prenatal care because I hid my pregnancy from my mother and father. I was so ashamed, scared, and guilty even though, I was a grown-ass woman, who had graduated high school at the age of 17. I went to a business college and got my certificate in executive secretary while pregnant. I also graduated early with a "B" average because I knew I was pregnant. When my mother found out everyone was so mad and upset that I was pregnant. I felt I had let my whole entire family down. I felt like the great white hope we had failed and lost the fight. This was a tremendous burden on my heart.

Even if the burden was not spoken out loud it was an internal known factor. It was heavy on my shoulders and I knew I had made a mistake and according to my raising I knew better. I also felt I had let God down my having sex before marriage and allowing myself to become pregnant which was definitely against the way I was raised. I carried such a severe burden and pain until I felt the pain was going to kill me. But I kept on praying through the pain and the tears. I got a little better each day. Three months later, I got hired at NMMC Hospitals as a wards secretary. This was one of the best things that had happened to me and it kept me from grieving so hard and kept my mind occupied. I became interested in nursing during this time and I would finish my paperwork and errands so I could go in the room and talk to the patients whom I fell in love with. I decided to go to nursing school the following year in January 1980. I graduated from nursing school in May 1982.

My Baby Girl

To my baby girl, on 8/8/1984 when GOD blessed us with you, your daddy was down there watching you come out and he had these big white beautiful teeth and all 32 was showing and the doctor and nurses were smiling at him because he was so excited!! You were our first after loosing Sabrina and I was sooo excited but scared and automatically went into protective mode!! I remember you looking just like your sister and I literally had to see you breathe at night!! In my mind I could never allow anything to happen to you and at night your daddy slept with you on his chest because he knew how I felt and he felt the same way. We had to hear you breathe!!

We were so proud of you. All I wanted was for you to grow up and become a strong woman who is self-sufficient and educated and able to take care of yourself. And to God's glory you exceeded all of my dreams and aspirations for you. You have made a beautiful family with MURRIO and my Sugarbear MJ, and you have become the strongest young woman I know. I love you guys with all my heart!!

Your Mom

My Baby girl and Son-in-Love

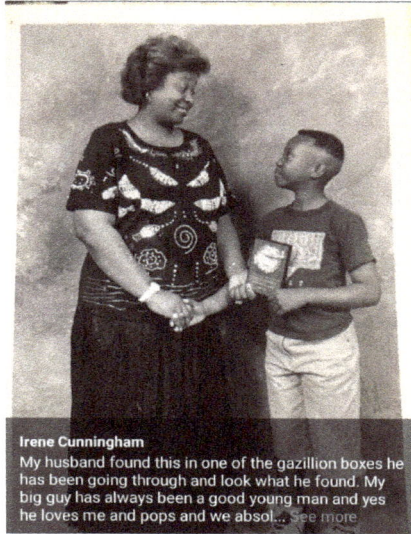

Irene Cunningham
My husband found this in one of the gazillion boxes he
has been going through and look what he found. My
big guy has always been a good young man and yes
he loves me and pops and we absol... See more

J.R. My Big Guy

Dear J.R., My Big Guy,

I became pregnant with you 8 months after your big sister was born!!! Again we were nervous and sooo excited because this meant we would have two babies at once!!! On 1/3/1986 you were born and weighed 7lbs 11oz and you had this head full of curly black hair and the prettiest boy I had ever seen. Words cannot express the love I had for you and I knew your sister would be jealous of you because she was spoiled rotten and was our whole focus for 18 months. She scratched you on your leg your first day home so I knew we had to watch her with you. Then as you grew up you two became best friends and inseparable. You started walking early to keep up with your sister and you were so bow-legged that a pig could run through your legs. But you grew out of it and have continued to be the most respectful, kind, loving child a mom could have. You favor me a little but you have all of your daddy's ways and as a young man you never wanted to talk loud to me and love me in spite of me being me. You married the love of your life last year and you two have planned your life and you are following your dreams!!! I hope you and Toya have the life that me and your dad prayed for you to have. I can't wait for more grandbabies!!!

Love you my son and my daughter-in-love Toya
MAY GOD BLESS YOUR UNION!!

What's the Value of A Black Man's Life?

My oldest son who has a Master's Degree in Computer Engineering Security at MSU recently told me about how he felt concerned about his accomplishments as a Black man does not matter.

In reality, he really broke my heart. Because he chose to stay in school 7 years and do the right thing so he can live a good life like we had afforded him. Its like he said none of that mattered. He said he feels like his life is not valued by America.

I definitely understand this. Especially seeing black men shot down in the streets even when they are running for their life.

He is my black Bill Gates....When I lost my baby boy, my eldest son told me, "Momma, I don't feel like my life means anything. " My baby! He has a Master's Degree in Computer Engineering Security. He should be Bill Gates. He is the black Bill Gates to me. I could not leave this world without saying something.

About Joshua's Poem

Hello my family and friends, I put this poem in my story because my late son, Joshua Tyler Cunningham, wrote this poem for me on Mother's Day when he was 6th grade, and my husband, my lover, and my best friend found it while going through some of his things. I needed this today to remind myself of the LOVE I have for him and my never-ending love and dedication for my family. You know I know my baby boy loves me, but to see these words again, brings tears of joy to my eyes and made me give myself a hug. It took me five long years to say they are joyful tears. In his own words he said everything a child should say to their parents, and to know that he knew I had his back no matter what! Lord in heaven knows I have cried so many sad tears.

I miss my baby driving me crazy, I would do anything to have him here with me today. But as a woman who loves GOD and knows that GOD'S will shall be done, I know weeping endures for a night but JOY comes in the morning.!!!!!! I have always known that, but putting that into perspective and being able to accept losing your baby is a whole other level. So in conclusion, I will continue to honor GOD who is the head of my life, and thanking Him for keeping me here and keeping me in my right mind.

AMEN AMEN AMEN!!!!!

Joshua's Poem

MORE THAN A MOTHER

When God set the world in place , when he hung the stars up in
space
When He made the land and the sea, then he made You + Me
He sat back + saw all the was good, He saw things to be as they
should
Just 1 more blessing he had in store,
He created a mother, but what for.
He Knew a mother would have a special place , to-shine his
reflection on her child's face
A Mother will walk the extra mile, just to see her child

She'll work her fingers to the bone, to make a house into a home.
A mother is there to teach + guide a mother will stay right by
your side
She'll be through your pain and strife, she'll stay constant in
your life
A mother will lend a helping hand , until-you have strength to
stand
She'll pick you up when you're down, when you need a friend she'll
stick around
A mother is one who listens well , will keep her word , will
never tell
A mother never pokes or pries , but stands quietly by your side
Giving you strength you need, encouraging you to succeed.

A mother is one who can be strong, when you need someone to
lean on
You're more than a mother to me; A reflection of him in your face
I see
A love that has no boundaries
I'm glad that you chose to be, all this and more to me
You share a love that knows no end
you're more than my mother, you are my friend

Raised in Fear

Things I dealt with number one is fear, being raised in the fear of the boogeyman for example is how as a child I began to develop fear of the unknown. In the room next door, hearing a noise outside, and being told the worst scary stories ever as a child. It felt and sounded real. Guilt, anger, shame and pain are other things I dealt with.

I realize now, I was living with P.T.S.D., a type of fear of anything happening to our children, especially after Sabrina passed away.

I was married to my first love and I was going to have my kids for one man and one man only. Because children have to pay for that and they become pawns in a game for some folk. I wanted a stable life for them. I knew I had to choose the life I wanted for our children.

PAIN COMES IN MANY WAYS....

Pain can come in many ways such as physical, mental which includes emotional spiritual Etc psychological pain can be just as severe as physical pain.

20 Years of Pain, Shame & Fear

20 years of pain shame and fear laying in my bed looking on-line and doing some paperwork, it is 3:30 a.m. and I realize it has been over 20 years since I work as an RN. I realize that I have made decisions in my life based on my beliefs in how I was raised to never leave your husband and kids no matter what. This was something my mom had always instilled in me, that even if me and my husband didn't make it, or you lose a job, you can never leave your children, no matter what price you have to pay. And I believe those words with all my heart because she not only said those words but she lived those words.

One day, I asked her, " Mom why are you still here and you say you are angry with my dad, for the things he has done to you?" She looked at me and said,

"I had nine little children and I would never allow another man to come into my life and be over my children."

She knew deep down she was truly in love with my dad, and I realized it earlier in my life as a small child. But her reasoning made sense, because with five girls you run the risk of bringing a man in your home over your girls, and a growing boys, would probably be in conflict with another man coming in over their mother. So she said to raise my children and I stayed with their daddy. Even though I know, some women have to leave relationships for reasons like abuse and cheating. As a young woman of 19 years old, I fell in love with the nursing profession. I was working at my first job at N.M.M.C. after our first child's death. I had been to business college and received an executive secretary diploma in June 1978.

I was four months pregnant but my parents or siblings did not know. That was a secret I could not let out. But my husband knew and so did his mother. I was so ashamed for getting pregnant because I was taught no sex before marriage. And in those days you were shamed so severely for having a child out of wedlock. I was so afraid to tell my parents and so ashamed of how my family would see me. It was like I had killed someone.

March 26th 2020 ENTRY

I always wanted my kids and husband to be proud of me. When I returned to college, I started to have all of these issues occurring in my life all of a sudden, I was in a dream one minute. I was in school full-time 12-hour semesters working 72 hours every two weeks taking care of three kids on honor roll, helping take care of my mom and dad, helping raise my nieces and nephews, helping my family and friends with their problems finances and or medical.

By 1998, I had lost three nephews one murdered in Parchman Mississippi and one nephew shot straight through the heart and I was the supervisor that night when he was brought in to my ER. I saw him on the screen and thought, "Lord have mercy Margaret, wonder whose child that is being carried in?" I got downstairs and the paramedic was removing his shirt and I saw the diamond ear-rings in his ear, and those little poochie lips and as his shirt was being brought over his face I said,

"Jimmy that's my nephew, 17 years old!" Jimmy said,

" Alright Irene you know what you have to do."

I sucked it up got that 18 gauge IV catheter and popped it in his vein. His blood was so dark dark red. I knew he only had a slow Rhythm and I popped and amp of atropine in his veins and his heart picked up and I screamed,

"Lord let's get the helicopter and transfer him to the trauma center NMMC!" But the doctor said,

"Irene I am afraid it would not do any good. Because," he said, then Jimmy raise them up so we could see his back, I saw a huge round hole on his back. I could not realize at that time that he had no chance because he was shot point-blank straight through his heart. I shook my head and said I have to call my brother and his mom. That was hard having another nephew dead for no reason. Lord have mercy I got to hold up and be strong for my family Psalms 91 personal time.

And then, my same brother lost another son. He went missing under suspicious circumstances and we never knew the whole story behind his life and death. But I remember my big brother prayed and asked God to bring his son home, and He did.

Some may wonder why is she giving all that information, I am telling my children what I have been through just in case I am not here when they become adults, they will know.

But again, God brought me through again and He continues to keep me.

Thanks be to God for all you have done for me.

Being Raised in Guilt

Being raised in guilt, is when you have been made to feel guilty for any and every little thing that the family taught was wrong can be hard on you. For example, when I was in third grade, I ate a pack of donuts, while walking around in the store. I was eating in front of everyone including the owner, I didn't go outside the store. At the time, I knew was wrong for eating the donuts but they were so juicy and fresh and the icing was creamy and I could not resist them. My sister saw me and told my mom. I was told it's so bad and made to feel so awful. She gave me the quarter to pay for the donuts and told me to go back apologize and ask for forgiveness. I felt so guilty and ashamed but I had to do it or get beat to death. I feel deep down that I was not wrong but I could not argue or go against what my parents said. SMH

SHAME-FACED...

There is a word we used back in the day known as shamefaced. In reality it's what they call you if you look down and acted shy especially when someone spoke to you or looked at you. It's also when you eat the donuts and you know you're not supposed to. Shame can also be carried into adulthood and can become a block in your life and keep you from moving forward. As I get older, it becomes less visible, but it can hold you back in many ways. I know I must let go of the shame, pursue my dreams, and complete my future endeavors. I will never stop dreaming because my God has everything I need.

No More Procastination

No Procrastination! No Getting Discouraged! Stay the Course!

I have procrastinated in the past and I refuse to be deterred anymore. For whatever reason, I know what I want. But I keep on waiting. I also get discouraged sometimes, but I have to stay encouraged in order to meet my goals. I must stay the course that I have started and will complete my classes one day at a time. I pledge to myself, that I will work hard and stay the course. I will complete my Bachelor's degree and my Master's Degree, by any means necessary. ONE DAY AT A TIME!!!

Family Matters

I was talking to my daughter a few days ago and we were discussing how we were raised and how we raised them (our children).

I made decisions about 20 years ago to come home and raise my family after lengthy discussions with my husband, my ride or die. This would be one of the best things I did when my kids were young.

I put in my resignation and continued taking classes toward my B.S. N. to become a FNP. After things started to settle, I was faced with mental, physical, financial, psychological things going on. I decided to stop working. Jackson had given me an ultimatum to work down there for 6 weeks to 6 months. I was told by my husband that he would take care of me as he had always done and would continue to do. I realized long before this that my husband was sent from above but it was more than solidified at this moment. He is my backbone and he truly loves me unconditionally.

At this time my baby was about 6 years old. All I know during this time was I had to put our children first and I could not leave them any no period of time. I realized that my mom and dad were old and not able to take care of my children. Because of the family on both sides I know we made the correct decision.

We both said before our children were born that they would be our first priority, no matter what the circumstance, always put your babies first and God will bless you.

4

I AM TOTALLY DEFEATED 12/28/08

Sunday, December 28, 2008
12:00 Noon

It is finally time to admit to myself that I am totally defeated!!!
I AM DONE, FINISHED, TIRED, CONFUSED, AGITATED, IN PAIN, HURTING, SAD, EXHAUSTED, TIRED OF FIGHTING, AND READY TO ADMIT TO MYSELF THE SUPERMOM, SUPERWIFE, SUPERFRIEND, SUPERAUNT, ETC. that I am sick, I am vulnerable, nervous, anxious, tired of being in pain, tired of being sick, sick of being tired and I have got to get help!

I am surrounding with so many dysfunctional situations even though my family (my husband and kids)are the best things that ever happened to me. I am at the point where I question if I am the best thing for them. So being a woman who loves God I have to love my family enough to get help before I have a total breakdown.

I have been sick this time almost 3 weeks and my stomach feels like a knife is jabbing me right in the pit. It is time for me to get my life together, become a better wife, mother, and mainly a better person. This is who I am and have always strive to be a good person who wants to do better.

Love Irene

5

2 Days before New Years 12/30/08

It is two days before New Years Day. I am sitting here thinking about all my stuff. I am very stressed out, I am very anxious and don't even know why. I have a good life a wonderful husband and three strong-minded beautiful children.

I love my family so much and I want to be a better wife and mother. I want to again become the strong black professional woman that I used to be. I feel that I am dying inside and drowning in my own tears and I feel no one can understand. I have suffered physically for so long that It has totally took over my life. I live in pain everyday. I also have a lot of mental and emotional pain. I have been used and abused by my extended family and they think it is just OK!

It is like nothing ever happened. There are times when you cannot just forget about all the pain. Some time or another I have got to face my pain and intend to do it in the year of 2009.

NO MORE PAIN, JESUS is my MEDICINE.

Love Irene

December 28, 2022

Looking back over this post, I realize I was suffering the loss of my mother. I totally see where my pain was coming from at this time. Not only did I have the ongoing physical injury, but I lost my real friend whom I knew had my back no matter the circumstance. She truly loved her baby. S.M.H.

6

2009 Is Almost Gone

August 1, 2009

I was just sitting here reading my last entry and I realized that the year 2009 is almost gone. I am still trying to get over the pain, fear and anger. I must get to the core from which I was raised.

My mother was forty years old when I was born. She raised me to be strong, proud and to hold my head up no matter what happens. She raised me to believe that if you fall down, don't wallow in the mud, pick yourself up and clean yourself up and keep going. That is so simple that I was taught these things so early on and felt those were just old fashioned sayings from my mom. But these truths are so simple. If you fall down, don't wallow, pick yourself up, clean yourself up, and keep going. So, so simple.

In May 2008, on Mother's Day, my mother died. I miss her body but I feel her presence and her strength. I know what I must do for me. My youngest baby is in college, we have finally moved him out. He is an adult. It is my turn now.

I love you Lord

7

September 11, 2009

Today is a beautiful rainy day. Physical pain and mental pain as usual. I sit alone in my house day in and out trying to figure out how I got here. I was so people oriented and always had lots of people in my presence. Now it is just me, myself and I and that is O.K. Because now, I also realize that when there were many people around, they also had an agenda. They need something that you have, whether it is food, money, your knowledge, a shoulder to cry on, etc. But once they think I am down and out, I have no one not even my own family (extended). I still have my strong beautiful hubby, my kids. It is sometimes very hard to come to the realization that you have been used. But that's OK. Because what I have done for others comes from one place and one place only and that's from the heart. So I have no regrets.

Love Irene

*A Continuation from this journal entry...

I have also began to realize that a lot my physical pain comes from my mental pain and anguish. So, I must work on my mind first and then my body, then my spirit, then my soul, so I can become the real person I want to be. I do not want to continue to live a fake life and live a lie. I just want to be me, no less, no more, no better, no worse, just me.

Physically, I am suffering and I know where I have to begin. I am attacking my own body mentally and I suffer even more physically. I have many plans on how to carry out my healing but I just have to begin. I must start somewhere.

I am beginning to think about all the pain I have been through in my life. Overall, I can say I lived a good life. But as an adult, I realize now that by the age of eight, I was having to do "private duty" on my 80 year old grandmother. We had to leave our home every night to go stay with her and I now know that it was not the right thing for an eight year old child to do. My grandmother suffered with organic brain syndrome and most nights she would keep us awake with her ranting and raving and fighting. There were many nights my sister and I didn't sleep.

We were taught very early on how to do and care for others including our sick aunts, uncles, cousins etc. If my mother said to do it, you did not question it. I now realize I would not let my kids go through these types of things because I feel a child should be a child. They should be allowed to run and play at home and not live in fear and have to care for grown adults or old people.

The responsibility was so great at that age and as my grandmother's disease progressed we would have to physically hold and grab my grandmother to keep her from getting away. God help me and my sister if she had got away! We would have been beaten to death. As a mother, I always said I would never subject my kids to that type of trauma. I also realize as a woman, my mom had to work and take care of us. So that left me and my sister all day and everyday taking care of her and my nieces and nephews.

8

There is a time to be a child

There is a time to be a child and there is a time to be an adult. We had to go through this from the time I was eight until age eighteen. By this time my mom finally moved my granny out of her house into our house. So there was no relief, same thing in our house. I went to business college for one year and by the time I finished my one-year course, I was pregnant. I was six months pregnant with my oldest child Sabrina Marie Payne. She was born to Joseph and me on October 27, 1978, early that morning. She was a beautiful, healthy four pounds, premature baby. She was born at seven months. The next day she started to vomiting up her formula. The x-ray showed her intestines were not developed or connected from the upper to lower. She was sent two days after birth to LeBonheur Children Hospital, in Memphis. The pediatrician stated there was nothing they could do. She lived for five weeks and we brought her home and she passed away three days later in my mom's bed. I don't think I ever got over her death even to this day.

I remember Jospeh was standing right there when she passed away. His mom and aunt were right there too. It was so sad. SMH

Thank you Lord,

Irene

9

I graduated from nursing school in1982

I graduated from nursing school in May 1982. I went to State Boards and I passed on the first try! I was so proud of myself and so was my family. It was like becoming a Registered Nurse was making up for becoming pregnant before marriage. It is like I had redeemed my mistake. How sick is that? I started my job in May 1982 and moved out into my apartment in September 1982, during this time period of one year. I worked 12 hour night shift. I partied and dated other people and eventually Joseph and I got back together. He purchased me a house back in May 1983 and we got married in September 1983. Yes I married my first love. This was all I ever wanted was to have a good husband, a good job, and healthy children and eventually I had all three. I had my dream husband, my dream job and my healthy children who were also a dream come true. In my life it was my three loves. I never could have imagined during this period of my life that anything could go wrong, especially on my job. I loved my patients and I treated them like family. I always wanted to learn and study medicine and increase my knowledge and understand what I was doing and why I was doing it. I took classes also took a class at the "W", and I also took classes at Ole Miss in Gerontology and became certified in applied Geriatrics because of my love of older people.

I went to Atlanta in 1995 and took my test at Georgia State University to become one of not many to become ANCC certified in Medical/Surgical Nursing.

My title changed to Irene Cunningham, RNC!!! I was so proud of myself because I believed you should always continue to increase your area of specialties as an RN because you need to stay on top of your game in the nursing profession!!! There was backlash from it because one young man who was in Respiratory Therapy asked me what did the RNC stand for because he had never saw the "C" on any RNs name tag. I explained it to him and he looked and said oh ok! I explained to him that was one of my personal goals to become certified and it was not a requirement. I loved taking care of people.

10

First Black RN

I was the first black RN to study and become the Hemapheresis is Nurse to do plasma changes and single donor platelet procedures, while being a preceptor on the cancer floor at NMMC. I always had the wisdom and drive to be a better nurse to always give the best care possible to my patients. I can see my qualities and desire in my daughter who is an excellent nurse whom I greatly respect for her desire to do a great job at caring for her patients. I also have a niece who I respect as an RN and I am also proud of her. There are many great nurses but they are doing a wonderful job but I can see through my experience and from other people that they care for the total human is not the same. They feel nurses do not care the way they used to care about people.

11

Golden Rule

Somewhere along the way the genuine love for one another have gone and got lost. Most people in the nursing profession do not have empathy for their patients and go into nursing for the money. Nurses do not know the value these days of the white uniform and what it means to wear the white. The scrub generation has taken over. I cannot tell an RN from an NA from an X-ray tech, from a dietary worker. The Pride I felt when I put on my starched and ironed white crisp uniform was so great and I felt it meant clean, healthy and life. The pride of being a nurse has been lost. A new nurse should be taught that once you take that oath it is done with the ultimate responsibility to life and pride. They must be taught to have each other's back and if another nurse is in trouble or hurting we have to have empathy and sympathy and help one another out in any way we can. And of course, we must always remember to DO NO HARM, and this to me is the golden rule.

12

October 27, 2013

October 27, 2013, I cannot believe that this was the last time I made an entry into my diary. It has been three years. This gives you an idea about the true pain and heartache I was experiencing both physical and mental. But thank God Almighty I am still here this close Friday on 10/26/13 I had a life-altering experience. I got so sick I could not even see and there it is. Except for periods of circles of light and being able to see only through the circle, what was going on in the ER.

Love You God,

Irene

13

October 28, 2013

October 28, 2013, I do know deep in my heart that the experience God took me through on Friday. I saw all of my life during that time and felt God was dealing with me in a way I had never experienced before. It was like being brought back to life after a near-death experience. I could speak at the time and I kept saying to Joseph I love you baby and you have been so good to me. I was thinking to myself, what would Josh, J.R., and Candice feel and think, when I am gone. I was seeing MJ and thinking what is he going to do without his granny and what would he say.

Love You Lord

14

November 23, 2013

November 3rd 2013 I'm being judged I am so sick and tired of people judging me and other people. Why do we have to judge one another. Why can we not just accept one another for who we are and love each other unconditionally. We are not God so who are we as humans to judge others? All we need to do is support one another when needed and pray for God to help us make it through whatever we are experiencing at the time. It's just not necessary to judge. It makes you feel so isolated and alone. Even when a person says otherwise, it hurts, and what every person needs during their trials and tribulation is unconditional non-judgmental love.

15

Don't Lose Your Light

As a nurse, I have come to see or just realize that after a long period of time we lose our light. This light I am referring to is a Candlelight, lit so many years ago by Florence Nightingale. You remember the light you had when you dreamed of becoming a nurse when you were young and a time when you were admitted to nursing school and you can see yourself in that crispy white uniform and polished white nursing shoes. And then, that like when you're walking to your pinning ceremony and receive your school of nursing pin and you get for your first day of orientation as a graduate nurse and you go to state Boards of Nursing and see your RN license and start to walk the halls as an RN. The light am referring to is the light in your eyes, and the proud feeling you as if you can save the world of disease, pain, stress, and long-suffering. This is the light that we as nurses must take back to remind people, patients, and the public of why we are nurses and show them how we love and respect our position that we were blessed with by God. Because to me I felt so much pride and empathy and feel to be a nurse is me doing God's work. Just as we say cleanliness is next to Godliness, to me nursing is close to Godliness. We lose that light because of the many pressures and politics of Nursing. We become warped in the muck of the meds and mess and forget what our true call is to take care of the sick and dying and if possible, bring them back to Optimal Health! Depending on the circumstances, to the main part of being a good nurse, is the first " Do No Harm."

I was one of the nurses who broke myself down after almost twenty years up and down those Hospital halls doing my best to care for my patients. I have worked as Charge nurse, and Supervisor and many days and nights, I was the only RN in the whole hospital. I had to work with one LPN and run back and forth to the ER, Pharmacy, play MD until the doctor arrived, and even breathe for the patient if that was necessary at the time. So when you find yourself going through the motions and taking care of your husband, kids, patients, sisters, brothers, nieces, nephews, any and everyone, and even help friends. But in the meantime, I was not taking care of me, and this is when I lost my light. Some people may say you should have taken care of yourself first. In reality, you feel that you are doing what God and your parents want you to do and do not see 20 years down the road you will be a broken down, in pain physically, and mentally, and find yourself in a hole that God and only God can bring you out of. I have seen my friends who have passed away from cancer have numerous breakdown, lose their homes, families and everything they had worked for because of losing the light and letting their light burn out. We must first take care of ourselves so we can be better nurses, mothers, wives, daughters, sons, friends, and etcetera. This is the only way to get and maintain that light. There are many ways to take care of yourself first as a nurse. First we must take care of our basic needs and physical health. We must exercise regularly and eat good meals. We should start out taking care of our Mental Health from the beginning!!

Nurses must stay strong and if you lose it, take back your light. If a nurse hears this phrase and they don't understand it, they are not in nursing for the right reason. We as nurses need to be very strong for our families, and our patients who depend on us and so many many others who look up to you in the church, job, community and etcetera. We must also maintain the light which is the lantern lit many years ago by Florence Nightingale, who was nursing the wounded soldiers. I see that light as a smile when you walk in the patient's room and a gentle touch and a kind voice when you speak to the sick and wounded. They can make a great difference in that person's hospital stay or illness experience. That light shows the empathy which means putting yourself in the other person's place, and basically treat that person the way you would want to be treated.

For me this is the golden rule for the true nurse.

16

20 Years of Experience

But as a 20-year RN, I have experienced lots of things. And I will also inform any nurse that they should first shine the light on him or herself in order to be able to do all these things required for a nurse to be the best that she or he can be. And I can truly say that I lost my light!!

I let my job get into my personal life. I would bring my job home with me and be unable to forget about my 19-year-old cancer patient whom I was nursing for the last 2 to 3 months and he died while holding my hand. I let it get to me.

I can truly say I am guilty of being too human. But is that right? These words I can say, "that if my love and care of the sick is my downfall then I must pay the price," because I would not have it any other way. I can truly say that nursing is truly a love of my life, after God, family, and friends. I could never say I regret my life.

Because I can truly say I have had a blessed life. Even though I lost my first child, Ms. Sabrina Marie Payne. God blessed me three more times with Candace, JR, and Joshua, and I am still with my baby's daddy(smile) for thirty plus years, married and dated him for 10 years. And yes, I still love and I am still in love with him today. And I still have that spark for him even after all this time. Truly he has been my true reason for raising our children, being able to handle problems on my job, with my family, extended family and all other trials and tribulations I had to go through. He is my Earthly Rock and God knows that He is my Spiritual Rock, he prays for me. Had I not had a personal relationship with God oh, I know I would not have made it. He kept me and I am still here. And I have a beautiful grandson M.J. who I love and adore. And now we have Savannah B, our angel from God. So, as you can see, God Just Keep on Blessing me over and over again!

Thank You God!

17

February 9, 2014

February 9, 2014

Today I am sitting here on my bed, (Saturday)watching a re-run of any Iyanla Vanzant, "Fix My Life" and I realize each time I see this particular show, I see something or some little detail that I missed on a previous viewing. This part where she asked the lady in her house, about the baby she lost to crib death and I see her in me. Once you lose a child it affects who you are for the rest of your life and I thought to myself how I was told by my mother when I lost my first-born child to give it to God. She told me I had to get myself together because Sabrina was one of God's angels and that she was resting in heaven. After constantly crying on my bed tears of immense sadness and severe pain, I knew I had to let it go and try to suck it up and keep going. At that time, I felt like I could have cried a whole year and I would not have let out enough tears to equal the pain I felt for the loss of my little baby girl. I could cry at this moment, as I write these words on paper right here and now because of the pain of losing Sabrina.

You can never get over that loss, and if you do not deal with it, and get help at the time of your loss you will deal with it in some other crazy way during your lifetime. I have learned from experience that we should talk to some person, pastor, counselor or professional trained in the field of grief and loss. Because if you stuff it down and think it is over you will pay for that stuff one day. And it may be in a way that you would never believe you would. Right today, I realize I have not dealt with things of my childhood and adult issues that I had literally stuffed for 40 plus years. I realized that I have to deal with them for myself to heal and begin to live my life the way I should and dreamed of. I know I have done many things in order to get by and hold on. I'm seeing my three children God allowed me to raise become self-sufficient. So now the procrastination has to end. I must deal with my stuff so I can live and achieve my dreams. I have been so abundantly blessed with a very supportive loving husband who loves me so much, he and my three beautiful healthy children are my true love. And I am so blessed to become a grandmother. With you, MJ, I am so blessed by God and I have to heal my past wounds so I can enjoy the true Gifts of having raised my children and have a grandchild. I celebrate thirty plus years of marriage to the same man. I have only been married once and yes; all my children are by the same baby daddy. I can smile on that one cuz it is a true accomplishment for today when there is a 50% divorce rate in today's society. I know this is not an easy task but it can be done if you and your spouse fight for your family no matter what happens. You have to be strong when things go wrong in the marriage just as you are when things are going right. As a 39-year-old mother of three young children, I resigned from my position because I was injured severely on the job and was not willing to sacrifice my children for a job. I had to as their mother stay strong and come home and finish raising them while my husband told me he would take care of me and our kids if he had to work 7 days a week and 12 hours a day. And he did just that, and he never complained, he continued to support our children and me through everything they went for in their school years and through college.

This is my encouragement to be a better wife, mother, grandmother, sister, aunt, cousin, and friend. I was raised to no matter how far you fall to pick up yourself clean up yourself and keep on going. That is why I am writing these words to encourage other young women to never give up. Take care of your family and God will bless you. I am writing in my journal I am getting off my original thought smile. So again, sitting on my bed I'm thinking how did I get here at this juncture of my life. I have been disabled for over 10 years and I am still suffering from an initial injury to my lower back.

The condition that I have, is degenerative and it usually gets worse with time. I have my trust in the Lord and I will get better with time because I can do all things through Christ who strengthens me. God has my back!!!

18

Dear God, Thank You for My Pain

Dear God

Thank You for my pain

As I lay here in my bed, hurting as usual, I want to say thank you Lord. Thank you for my pain, thank you for the ability to feel my pain, because some people are paralyzed and cannot even feel their legs arms or any part of their body. I am praying for more and more strength and healing from God, so I can be of more help to others who are much more sicker than my back or leg pain. I want to just stop complaining because I know in my heart, I am truly blessed in spite of the pain I feel each and every day, I can say today I won't complain. But I truly want to make these three words my mantra I know my God in heaven loves me and has a job for me to do so it is high time for me to get on the job at hand. I am going to take this test one day at a time, and I know with God I can do anything. He will give me the strength to fulfill my heart's desire. So again, I say thank you Lord thank you Lord! Thank you, Lord! I

Just Want to Thank You Lord! I'm asking God and praying for the strength to study and show myself approved and do the job God put me here to do. And that is, helping others and loving my fellow man as God asked us to do for one another. And I do mean truly love unconditionally and give help to others who need it without expecting anything in return. This is how I have always lived but I have let my problem and my pain get in my own way. So, I have in my heart to get to work on me one day at a time dear Jesus.

19

True Forgiveness for Self

How I Must Began My Journey

to healing my body, mind, and soul. I have to go about these roads of healing one step at a time. My number one step is to first forgive myself for all of my selfish endeavors and then only after I forgive myself, I can begin to forgive others who have wronged me.

To forgive has to be my first step because when you are making a mistake during your illness, physical, and/or mental, you may not be able to see your own mistakes and you can hold on to the wrongs of others who have wronged you, even though you or others had no idea that a wrong has been done. Even though I am so aware that everyone makes mistakes, it easier said that done. One day at a time.

True forgiveness for self.

ROCK BOTTOM

I have to go through the grunge? Or the dirty dirty or the rock bottom, so I can truly grow the way God wants me to grow! Do I continue to stay in pain, depression, and anxiety and be angry because I gave everything to everybody. I gave my family (extended) friends, my patients and I tired to help in the best way I know how because if I followed the Golden Rule quote,unquote, and I did unto others as I would have them do unto me, then my momma told me everything would be alright. And when it is not alright and the people you are serving do not accept the service. You give and the same manner in which you gave it , you began to get angry with yourself for allowing yourself to be used, abused, disrespected and unappreciated. Then you go into the ROCK BOTTOM when you are really MAD, depressed, anxious, reclusive because you cannot deal with nobody else's SHIT!!!

And during these periods you are up and down with anxiety and depression and decide to give of yourself to those who appreciate you. For example, your immediate family-husband, children, and your parents only because in the end, Who Gives a SHIT about you and what you have done for them, even if you gave them your last money, furniture, cars, got people out of jail, etc. etc. etc.

So you see why I call this period over 10 years my Rock Bottom. But even in my rock bottom, I still assisted almost 10 young ladies, spending many hours studying with them to help them through RN school, including my daughter(smile). I smile here because I have never lost my love for my job and I wanted these young ladies to feel that I was never just in it for money or fame, but I loved my job taking care of the sick.

I know they felt it because each of these young ladies came to me because they trusted me and they knew my love for nursing and they trusted that I would only give them the correct information and procedures, that would only lead to the greatest possible outcome for their main purpose for being a nurse and that is to to take care of the sick and afflicted.

I have always read, studied,took classes, and keep up with new meds that were being brought to the medical field and it keeps me up on my knowledge by sharing with these beautiful intelligent, young women. Three of these young ladies are RN's working in Los Angeles & Fresno, CA, and all 3 of them have their BSN's and one have obtained NP (Masters) and one will finish her NP in a year (Masters) and one will get hers in the very near future. So even in my ROCK BOTTOM I was still being of service to those who needed my help and I have never regretted it. It's people like them who remind you not just verbally, but in their own way that I have to get back to living my life and helping others in the same way.

I love them for truly knowing Irene.

I Am Sorry to those Who I have Not been Available for...

They knew in their hearts and minds, who I truly am and this has always reminded me to never ever ever stop dreaming. And I do know of many relatives and friends (Ali, Margaret) etc. etc. etc (Laura)who know who you really are, who still remained the same no matter what I was going through and these are the people you can never forget. They are the people who, like my husband and kids, my parents, in laws, grands who never let me down. I love you all for it even if I did not act like it all the time. I went through many periods of not wanting to deal with other people's stuff, because now I have my own stuff I have to deal with so I stopped visiting my family because I could no longer take on their issues and my issues too. It was just too much drama on top of my own stuff. But I always said if you need me I will be there and there were times when I could not be there because of my own physical and mental pain. I felt sad many times and felt terrible about letting people down but I was just not able to be there for them at that time. I am sorry for anyone who may have felt left or let down by me. But had I been able I would have been there. I had to truly put all the ENERGY I had left to my husband and my kids. I didn't have any reserve. I was truly at my best for my kids, so they would get the best of what I was dealing with and I could be at my worst or Rock Bottom while they were at school or at Grandma or at a friend's house. It truly took every ounce of energy just to do what I had to do including deal with my elderly parents and grandparents because I had to be there for them.

It is just a given. I had no choice in this matter or situation because they were always there for me too and helped me to raise my kids through school age, junior, and high school. They helped them become who they are today.

Thank You Lord!! I give the Grace to my God for having them in my life.

20

Last Entry....

Lying in bed watching L'eandria singing in L.A. and it brought back 2019 to me when I went there on my family members' request because of my depression and grief over losing Josh. I did it and her partner said it was $20,000 to go there to work on me!!! I found out that was one of GOD'S LESSONS FOR ME! I really felt like an aunt-mother to this child and found myself in a mess, but I thank the Lord He brought me out, after bringing me through!!! I had to realize that family to me is different for some people, and how I value my extended family!! On this visit I felt very threatened and disrespected and violated!!! So, God revealed to me that I meant no more to them than a stranger on the street. I know GOD had to show me the reality of how I really was not valued like i felt i should have been!!! Because I would never leave them out there hanging, because of who they are to me!!I never thought my family would handle me like that because they know if I am called, I come no matter what the situation!! I felt like I was nothing to them but now I realize they are not me, and I can't expect them to do what

I did for them!!! I had to let it go and love them from where they are, and not what I want them to be or do!!

This was truly an eye-opening experience that the Lord revealed to me at this time…It really hurt me because I really felt like I meant a great deal to them, but GOD showed me I was just like a homeless person off the streets!!! It didn't matter how I always showed up and many times showed out for them!!! GOD had to show me how much I really meant to them!! At the end of the day, I will still be there for them if I am needed because my love for them has never changed and if I just happen to cuss them out it's probably because my feelings were hurt and not because I don't love you!!!

I also need to always acknowledge my black sugar for looking beyond all my faults and saw my needs.. He has truly shown me what true love really is because he never gave me any ultimatums or timelines or time limits, because suffering with depression, anxiety, and chronic pain is a cumulative situation, and in each of these conditions can singularly be debilitating, let alone all three together is a whole other situation.

Being raised as a strong black woman, I was raised to never stop, hold your head up and keep going but I realize in reality I know I am one woman trying to be everything to everybody and I never put myself first. But GOD knew what I needed was a strong man, to love me through all the trials, tribulations, trauma, pain, losses, and issues that I had to face along the way. He is a great guy who always think about me, and if I am okay or good, and if I didn't have a strong relationship with GOD I would not know how or why he showered down his blessings on me to cover me with a good man of GOD!!!

www.ingramcontent.com/pod-product-compliance
Lightning Source LLC
Chambersburg PA
CBHW041928260326
41914CB00009B/1216